How to Lead a Small-Group Bible Study

Beacon Small-Group Bible Studies

How to Lead a Small-Group Bible Study

by
Gene Van Note

BEACON HILL PRESS OF KANSAS CITY
Kansas City, Missouri

Copyright 1980
Beacon Hill Press of Kansas City

ISBN: 0-8341-0653-1

Printed in the
United States of America

Contents

Introduction		7
1	Value of a Small-Group Bible Study	9
2	What Should Happen in a Small-Group Bible Study?	13
3	How to Start a Group	18
4	Your First Session as a Group	22
5	The Key to Success: Group Commitment	26
6	The Importance of Leadership	30
7	How to . . .	35
8	Learning to Pray	40
9	"How to Use This Study Guide," by Wil M. Spaite	43

Introduction

Small-group Bible study is not new. Believers have been sharing in this unique expression of the Christian faith for nearly 2,000 years. It was part of the first joyous celebration of their victory in Christ, as Acts 2:42 reveals.

Of course, the format, and to some degree the content, of small-group Bible study has varied greatly across the years. Each generation has developed its own style— an expression of the hopes and fears that commanded its attention. Yet, there is a family relationship between the house-churches of the New Testament, John Wesley's class meetings, the cottage prayer meetings of the early 20th century, and today's small-group Bible study. A growing number of contemporary Christians have rediscovered this ancient form of sharing and Bible study and have adapted it to meet the challenge of these troubled years.

We live in a day when the historic landmarks are being obliterated by change. Perhaps never before in history has the world experienced such a wholesale challenge of traditional values. Add to this the radical adjustments brought about by science and technology, and the results have been dramatic. A debilitating insecurity has invaded our culture. The dominant mood of our age is loneliness.

People everywhere are lonely. In the pursuit of the elusive dream of success they have moved away from the friendly scenes of their childhood and the loving support of their families. They have paused at a way station, a necessary interlude on their way to happiness and achievement. In another year, or two, or three, they will move again to another city—a new environment, a new set of friends—and the loneliness increases.

And yet, deep in our inner being we sense that God has created us with a basic human need for close personal relationships. Many people are learning that this need can be met as they join with a few other people in a small group to apply the Bible to their lives.

The combination of a caring, supporting group studying the Bible together often brings a new joy in relationships, both with our friends and with our Heavenly Father. The result is a new security—the exhilaration of belonging. With it comes the strength to make spiritual conquests, with the help of the Holy Spirit. Often a discouraged believer finds the way to victory in the warm, supporting atmosphere of a small-group Bible study.

This book will consider the various aspects that are involved in leading a small-group Bible study. One point needs to be made as we begin: You do not have to be an expert to be an effective leader of a small-group Bible study. No diplomas are required; no certification is needed; membership in a professional society is not necessarily an advantage.

To be a successful leader of a small–group Bible study, all you need is a love for people, the confidence that the Bible is the Word of God, a desire to make some new friends, and an openness to people and the direction of the Holy Spirit. There are, to be sure, some things we can learn from the experiences of others. Many of those ideas, techniques, and procedures will be discussed in the following pages. May we allow the Holy Spirit to be our Teacher as we take a closer look at our subject, "How to Lead a Small-Group Bible Study."

1

Value of a Small-Group Bible Study

In this chapter we consider these questions:

A. Why should we have small groups studying the Bible?
B. Are small groups necessary?
C. How do you know if you are successful?
D. What is the relationship to traditional worship?

A. Why should we have small groups studying the Bible?

This question was answered in the introduction. Let's review what was said there.

The caring relationships that were common in families in an earlier generation have been, in large measure, severely damaged in our day. Families have been fragmented. The distance that separates them has stolen the support that was traditionally a part of the family structure.

The church has not been exempt from these cultural trends. "The impersonalization and depersonalization of our society has struck deeply into the life of the Church and robbed us of our heart and warmth. To love Jesus' way, we have to really know and really care about one another as persons. It is precisely the awareness of lost contact with others that has led so many to join or form groups."[1]

In a lonely world, small groups provide a safe place where we are cared for and understood.

B. Are small groups necessary?

Larry Richards responds by asking, "Can't Christians reach their potential without a small-group experience? This is a most deceiving question because we have to answer both yes and no. Yes, because a person does not have to be in a 'small group' to grow. No, because it's clear from Scripture that no believer can reach his potential *alone*."[2]

Obviously, there is nothing magical about a small group. Nor is a small group necessarily more religious than a large congregation or a single individual. A small group can be a clandestine meeting of conspirators that destroys the Christian fellowship. However, when a few Christians join together to study the Bible and sincerely care for each other, God meets with them in a special way.

Perhaps the key question is, "Would it help me if I could develop a closer relationship with some other Christians?" If the answer is yes, then a small-group Bible study could be extremely valuable for you.

C. How do you know if you are successful?

This is an important question, but not an easy one to answer. At its core is the awareness that a group can fail.

Success is not automatic.

"A small group Bible study," writes Gladys Hunt, "gives people an opportunity to open the Bible in a neutral environment and discuss what it says. It provides a natural bridge into spiritual issues, to consider the meaning of life, the person of Jesus Christ. . . . It is not a preaching opportunity; it is a cooperative adventure in discovery."[3]

A small group studying the Bible together operates on the basic assumption that it does not need a resident expert to understand God's Word. Nor does it need a captain of the militia to guard the integrity of the truth. It believes that the Holy Spirit will guide earnest, sincere seekers to the Truth as they openly study the Bible. The leader, then, is not a Moses coming down off the thundering mountain with a divine proclamation. He is a Joshua, standing with his friends at the border of the Promised Land, saying, "Come on, fellas, let's see what God has for us today!"

This is not to imply that a successful group will treat the Bible carelessly. Together they soberly accept the responsibility to understand the Scripture and apply it fully and correctly to their lives.

A small group can consider itself successful when in a comfortable, natural way it experiences the presence of the risen Christ guiding them to a greater love for their Lord and each other.

D. What is the relationship to traditional worship?

The small-group Bible study is not a substitute for the regular worship services of the organized church. Seen in perspective, each brings out the best in the other. When Christians gather to worship having experienced a time of spiritual refreshing during the week, everyone is benefited.

On the other hand, we need times of great celebration when all the Christians of a particular fellowship join together in praise and rejoicing. These moments of celebration that come when the church is at worship lift us out of the routine and the ordinary. They inspire hope and bring renewal and peace.

The small-group Bible study needs to be closely related to the entire ministry of the church to draw from its high moments of celebration and return to it a measure of the inspiration and joy experienced in the between-Sunday time of sharing and Bible study.

2

What Should Happen in a Small-Group Bible Study?

In this chapter we look at the three main components of an effective small-group Bible study:

    A. Discussion Bible study
    B. Sharing experiences
    C. Praying together

We consider also the importance of:

    D. Constructive group tension

A. Discussion Bible study

There are a great many ways to study the Bible—and all of them are profitable. Not all of them are equally valuable in every situation, however. The selection of a specific study method should be determined by the goals toward which you are headed. Creative and vigorous discussion of God's Word is one of the most important parts of a redemptive small-group Bible study.

Discussion Bible study involves each individual at the level of his interest and understanding. It elicits participation and encourages spiritual growth through dialogue. This approach takes advantage of the maturity and experience of the group members. The different perspectives provide new approaches to understanding the Word. The interaction of a small group can open the way for the quiet and the troubled to ask questions about the meaning of specific Bible passages.

To be effective, a discussion group:
1. Must not be dominated by one person—either as the leader/teacher, or an expert who parades his knowledge.
2. Must have something to talk about other than private prejudices and opinions. Study of the Bible passage before coming to the session is extremely important.

A successful discussion group:
  —Provides an incentive for people to complete their personal Bible study on a regular basis.
  —Enables people to go beyond the limits of their own personal findings by exposing them to the ideas of others.
  —Creates an atmosphere which is conducive to honest sharing of personal discoveries, questions, problems or needs.
  —Fosters positive Christian fellowship where group members can develop solid personal relationships in an informal setting.
  —Equips young growing Christians with a method of helping others grow spiritually.[4]

B. Sharing experiences

"We don't say, 'Amen,' in church as often as we used to," a friend said to me one day. He continued, "We have lost something special. An occasional 'Amen' not only encouraged the preacher, it also alerted the congregation. If I was not really listening carefully to the sermon and a friend I respect said, 'Amen,' I began to wonder, 'What did I miss?' It alerted me to give the speaker my full attention."

Something akin to that happens when believers begin to share what the Bible is saying to them, personally. The Bible becomes fresh and alive. It takes on a new meaning and power in their lives because of the openness of another member of the group.

A good place to begin sharing is to use a Bible study method that has come into prominence in recent years. As you read the Bible passage, each person asks himself these three questions:

—What does the passage say?
—What does it mean?
—What does it mean to me?

As the trust-level increases in the group, individuals will welcome an opportunity to share their joys and their sorrows, their victories and their defeats. Ultimately, they may want to ask the help of the group at the point of their greatest spiritual challenge.

A small-group Bible study is not a therapy group. There are, of course, some personal experiences that ought not to be revealed. But as the group demonstrates its desire to be redemptive in their love and caring, people will sense that they can open up their lives without injury. No one needs to try and force any kind of public disclosure. When people begin to trust one another, they will welcome the opportunity to have someone help carry their burdens.

C. Praying together

Allow time for prayer. Personal communion with God is essential in all fruitful Bible studies. Determine to make prayer more than a "nod to God" at the beginning and end of each session. As members participate in sincere, unhurried prayer, you will be amazed how God's power will meet needs in your group—today!

In a later chapter in this book we will consider this theme in greater depth (see Chapter 8—"Learning to Pray"). At this point, it is important to recognize that prayer ought to be included as a significant feature every time the group meets.

D. Constructive group tension

Do not be surprised if people disagree. And don't panic. When people from widely different backgrounds come together, difference of opinion is inevitable—and beneficial. It is highly probable that the most creative sessions will be sparked by a major disagreement over an emotional issue. In a word—tension.

Most of us shy away from any form of tension in the church because of its potential for destruction. However, properly guided, tension can be the springboard for spiritual growth.

The pivotal question is, "How can the leader keep the tension from producing animosity, or anger, or any other negative emotion that would destroy the fellowship in the group?" Here are a few suggestions:

—The leader can remind the group that the Word of God is the final authority.
—Encourage participants to listen carefully to what others are saying.
—Change the mood from accusation to personal revelation. Use phrases like "This is what I think," instead of "You always . . ."
—Agree that not every difference of opinion must be resolved by everyone coming to the same conclusion. "Agree to disagree."
—After sufficient time has been given to the dis-

cussion of the disputed subject, interrupt the conversation by saying, "There are some major differences of opinion that we probably cannot resolve in this session. Let's take some time to think about what has been said and discuss it at a later session."

Occasionally, people ask the question, "Are small-group Bible studies safe?" One experienced leader responds, "As safe as life with Jesus always is. He sometimes takes us on great adventures and into water over our heads, but He is always there. The idea of changing people through personal encounter with God is His idea. We can expect Him to be present each time we gather."[5]

3

How to Start a Group

In this chapter, we take a look at the process of getting a group started. Our attention is focused on these important factors:

A. Identify the reason why you want to organize a small group.
B. Work closely with your pastor.
C. Make certain that it is open to the world.
D. Find interested people.

A. Identify the reason why you want to organize a small group

There are many legitimate reasons for participating in a small-group Bible study. Here are some of the reasons people have given for wanting to be a part of such a group:

1. Personal spiritual growth
2. In-depth Bible study
3. Fellowship
4. Evangelism and outreach
5. Finding answers to specific problems
6. Making new friends
7. Developing some close friendships
8. Helping new Christians

Your reason for wanting to organize a small-group Bible study may be one of those listed, or a combination of several of them. The list does not include all the legitimate reasons. Yours may not be there, but that does not make it any less important. As noted earlier, however, a clear concept of where you want the group to take you is a major factor in its success.

Clarify your thinking by writing in one or two sentences what benefits you would like to derive from the new group. This is the basic foundation stone on which to build.

B. Work closely with your pastor

The spiritual growth experienced by the participants in a small-group Bible study can be conserved most effectively when the group functions as a part of the total church. The goal is not to compete with the established church, but to provide an additional opportunity for spiritual enrichment for the worshipers. In addition, those new believers won to Christ through the group's care and concern, will need to become a part of the larger fellowship of the church.

Nor would any person who is interested in his church want to give the impression that the group has become a center for gossip and dissent. For these reasons, and others, keep your pastor fully informed of your desire to organize a small group to study the Bible together. You would, of course, be open to the leadership of the local church and develop the group in keeping with the total program of that local congregation.

C. Make certain that it is open to the world

The most effective safeguard to insure that the Bible study does not degenerate into a review of church problems is to make sure that some nonmembers attend every meeting. Their presence will help keep the group tuned in on Bible study. In addition, the freshness of their different viewpoint will provide an unexpected benefit.

It would certainly be contrary to the Christian mission for Bible study to be restricted to a group of church members who meet regularly at other religious events—in a word, a clique. Invite new people to experience the power and joy of the life in Christ that believers experience in the Spirit.

D. Find interested people

"The tendency in the beginning," observes Gladys Hunt, "is to search out all the Christians available and gather them into the study. And while that may be worthy and conscience-salving, it doesn't meet the needs of people around us who still don't know what they need to know about Jesus Christ. We need to say to our friends, 'This book is changing my life. Come and study it with me!'"[6]

1. How many people do you need to start?

We worship at the throne of bigness in these days. Statistical growth is the yardstick of success. And yet, Jesus said, "Where two or three are gathered together in my name, there am I in the midst of them" (Matt. 18:20). This verse of scripture has been used, too often, as an excuse for a small crowd on a rainy night. It is, in reality, a divine word on how many people are needed to begin.

It can be argued effectively that eight people make a more inspiring group than two. It is certainly true that ideal conditions make any experience better. But life rarely provides ideal conditions. The important thing is not how many, but when. Begin where you are—begin now!

2. Finding possible participants

Will everyone be interested? No, but some will be,

and you don't need many. There are a great many ways to recruit participants for a small-group Bible study. Here are some that have been used effectively.

(a) Social friends
(b) Colleagues at work
(c) Acquaintances at church
(d) Neighbors
(e) Distribute an advertising flyer in your block and hold an informational coffee hour
(f) Advertise: one effective leader placed an occasional ad in the neighborhood newspaper
(g) Ask the pastor for suggestions

"We need to get to the people who need to hear the message. They work and live in the areas where believers work and live. The people most likely to reach them are their peers. We cannot push our responsibility to witness off on the minister. The best way to reach them is by exposing them to an honest investigation of what the Bible says about God, about man, and about redemption."[7]

What a joyous opportunity to be a part of God's plan to bring His peace to the world.

4

Your First Session as a Group

In this chapter, we discuss:

A. The importance of the first session
B. The *Beacon Small-Group Bible Study Guides*
C. The need to create the right atmosphere
D. The role of the group in setting its own goals

A. The importance of the first session

It is probably not possible to overemphasize the significance of the first meeting of your group. First impressions are lasting. In your preparation try to put yourself in the situation of the one who is a stranger to most of the people, or the one who has had the least experience with this kind of event. Ask yourself how you would feel when you walked into the room. Try to anticipate the needs of each person in order to make them as comfortable as possible.

Name tags are often helpful. Print them plainly with both first and last names large enough to be seen at a distance.

Prepare yourself spiritually by spending time in prayer. You may also want to enlist some prayer partners who will support you in prayer as you begin.

B. The *Beacon Small-Group Bible Study Guides*

The *Beacon Small-Group Bible Study Guides* are designed for each participant to have one as an aid to his/her personal and group Bible study. These guides have been written to combine the three main components of each session: discussion Bible study, shared experiences, and a time of prayer. A variety of learning techniques are suggested in each book. This makes it easy, even for the untrained leader, to guide the group as it studies a specific book of the Bible.

For a list of current titles available in the Beacon Small-Group Bible Study Series, write for information to:

> Beacon Hill Press of Kansas City
> Box 527
> Kansas City, MO 64141

Determine, in advance of your first meeting, the book you wish to study. Order sufficient copies so they can be distributed at that first session.

C. The need to create the right atmosphere

There are many aspects that contribute to a successful Bible study. Some are very religious, like prayer and faith. Others are quite human and are easily overlooked because they don't appear to be very important. If ignored, however, they can make group Bible study difficult, if not impossible. Distractions like crying babies, television, and even barking dogs can interfere with the group's ability to give their best to each other and to the Word of God.

Give attention to practical details, such as these:[8]

1. *Meet in a comfortable, attractive place.* It does not have to be elegant or fancy, but it should be clean, warm, and friendly.

2. *Make appropriate physical arrangements.* It is imperative that you arrange the chairs in a circle. People need the face-to-face contact. Be alert to the special needs of anyone you expect to attend. Decide, in advance of the first meeting, how you plan to arrange the seating so you will not lose time or appear unprepared after people arrive.

3. *Maintain good lighting.* Adequate lighting not only makes it easier to read the Bible and the study guide, it contributes to a feeling of warmth and friendliness.

4. *Provide proper ventilation.* This is very important, but easy to overlook in planning.

5. *Anticipate and eliminate any distractions* such as television, loud stereo music, crying babies, pets, and unnecessary interruptions by children.

These suggestions may not cover all your needs, but they are examples of the kinds of practical matters that aid a group to reach its goals.

D. The role of the group in setting its own goals

In Chapter 3, "How to Start a Group," we suggested that you begin by identifying the reason you wanted to organize a group. At this point, the people that have come together for the first meeting need to establish ownership of the Bible study. That is, it should become "our group," rather than "Bill's Bible study," or the "group that Oscar leads."

The group can get involved in setting its own goals by referring them to section II, in the introduction at the

front of each Bible study guide.* That section is reproduced here.

Ask each person to consider the following:

One thing I would like to gain from sharing in this
time together is:

Rank the following in order, using number one (1) to
indicate the most important and number five (5) as least
important.

( ) 1. Learning to know Bible truths and apply
them to my life

( ) 2. A chance to begin all over again in my spiritual life

( ) 3. To grow in my personal faith in God

( ) 4. To deepen my friendships with others in
the group as we study the Word together

( ) 5. Other purpose _____

Take time to go around the group to introduce yourselves. Then let each member share what he or she would
like to gain from this Bible study by filling in the blanks
and by discussing this statement: I choose _____
as number one because _____. I put
_____ as number five because _____.

At this point, pause for prayer, asking God to bless
this Bible study and especially to meet the needs just
expressed by the members of the group.

When the members of the group take the time to set
their own goals, it not only establishes ownership, it
serves as a means to evaluate progress and a control to
keep the group on target. In later sessions, it may prove
to be a helpful tool, enabling the leader to bring the
group back from the discussion of a disruptive side issue.

---

*It will be helpful to your group spirit and study processes if each member
will read the introduction that appears at the front of his Bible study guide. See
Chapter 9 for a reproduction of the introduction by Wil Spaite.

5

The Key to Success: Group Commitment

This chapter is an expansion of the key idea in Chapter 4, section D, "The role of the group in setting its own goals." The climactic act of goal setting should be a group commitment. "The delight of a functioning small-group Bible study is that it has 100% participation. There is a commitment to group involvements. This is not a spectator sport, everyone gets into the action. And participation means that individuals have the joy of discovery."[9]

Here are some key items that should be included in the group commitment. Refer your study group to the introduction in each *Beacon Small-Group Bible Study Guide*.

A. Agree to make regular attendance a top priority of the group

Commitment to participate on a regular basis is crucial.

B. Where and when will the group meet?

Decide on a place and time for the meeting. The place can be always in the same home or in a different home each week, at a restaurant, or in any other relaxed setting where privacy can be assured.

The day of the week and the established time should not be changed from week to week except when absolutely unavoidable.

The group will also need to decide whether to meet every week, every other week, or according to some alternate schedule. Most people have discovered that a weekly meeting is most conducive to building a caring fellowship.

C. Decide on the length of the meetings

The minimum time length should be one hour; maximum two hours. Consistent attendance will be encouraged if you start and stop on time. If people wish, they should feel free to remain after the group is dismissed. However, by maintaining a careful time schedule, people can plan other aspects of their lives more easily.

D. Leadership

Decide whether the same person will lead each session, or if the responsibility will be rotated among group members.

The Beacon Small-Group Bible Study Series is prepared to allow for rotating leadership with a minimum of confusion. There are a number of good reasons for rotating the leadership throughout the group:

1. Divides the load.
2. Increases participation.
3. Expands the understanding of the importance of everyone sharing in the meeting.

4. Involves the new people and the quiet ones.
5. Tends to discourage one person from dominating the discussion.
6. Brings in new ideas.
7. Encourages preparation before coming to the session. The leader appreciates those who have studied the lesson.
8. Shares the joy of discovery. The leader always learns the most.

If the group should decide to rotate the leadership among themselves, then it will be helpful to select a coordinator. This person would take care of the practical and routine details related to the regular meetings.

E. Agree together that there shall be no criticism of others

No discussion of church problems, no gossip, and no criticism shall be expressed in the group. The goal is to affirm and to help each other mature in the Christian experience. This important concept will be discussed in more detail in Chapter 7.

F. Size of the group

Decide on the maximum number of people your group should contain. This is not to imply that groups should not grow. Welcome new people. Integrate them into the group as they understand and agree to the group commitment. This will add freshness and excitement to the meetings.

Experience has shown, however, that it is important to keep the group small. When the group gets to be larger than 10-12, then it is time to consider splitting into two smaller groups.

Why? Because "if the group grows too large, all the values of being a small group decrease: fellowship becomes less intimate, personal involvement diminishes, stimulation to prepare and opportunity to share lessons and the atmosphere becomes less of a group of close friends and more of a committee meeting."[10]

G. Preparation

The group meetings will be more fulfilling if each person completes his personal Bible reading before coming to the session.

H. Number of sessions

How many weeks is this Bible study group going to meet?

The group commitment is printed in the introduction to each study guide. It is reproduced below. After a careful period of discussion where the group has set its own goals, lead the group in completing this commitment:

MY COMMITMENT TO CHRIST
and THE MEMBERS OF MY GROUP

I agree to meet with others in my group for ____ weeks to become a learner in God's Word.

I commit myself to give priority to our group gatherings, to a thoughtful reading of the Bible passages to be explored, and to love and support others in my group.

Signed _____ Date _____

6

The Importance of Leadership

In this chapter, we give our attention to learning more about:

     A. Anybody can be a leader
     B. Ground rules for effective leadership
     C. Discussion techniques that work
     D. Some hints to success

A. Anybody can be a leader

That's right! Without exception, anybody can be a leader.

To be sure, right at this moment, some people in your fellowship have greater skills in leadership than others do. There may be many reasons for this: more experience, greater opportunity, the benefit of training, home environment, personality, etc. Our human tendency is to always ask the same people to lead—but anybody can be a leader.

Even at the end of the Bible study, some will be more gifted in leadership than others. It is important to remember that the success of the group is not dependent on a strong leader but on the full participation of the group. Being given the opportunity to lead may be a great encouragement, sparking spiritual growth in an unprecedented fashion.

If you are asked to lead one or more sessions of your Bible study group, don't automatically respond, "I can't do that!" Norma Spande asks, in this context,

"Does God ever ask us to do things we consider impossible? You bet He does. And as we respond to Him our faith grows (see Ephesians 3:20)."

Then she adds, "Put aside your mental picture of yourself as 'leader' and try to think of yourself as a tool that can be used in a variety of ways to reach others for Christ."[11]

Every person is different. That means that their leadership style is unique to them. We do not have to copy anyone else. Nor should we. We do not have to be a preacher or a prophet. All we need is the profound conviction that God has spoken in the book we call the Holy Bible. Couple that with the desire to learn and to share what God is doing, and it is clear—anybody can be a leader.

B. Ground rules for effective leadership

1. Stick to the chapter or passage under discussion.
2. Decide to avoid tangents.
3. Commit yourself to participate.
4. Start and stop on time (a vital rule).
5. Allow the Bible to speak for itself.
6. Use modern translations.
7. Come as you are.
8. Adopt this rule: no one will be asked to read or pray aloud without being consulted first.
9. Keep a good dictionary on hand; a good map is another handy study tool.

10. Don't bring commentaries to the study. Use them at home.
11. Learn to handle difficulties wisely. [see Chapter 7, "How to . . ."][12]

Remember, the Bible is your Textbook. Encourage careful reading of the passage to be discussed. Use the three important questions:

1. What does the Bible say?
2. What does it mean?
3. How can I use it?

C. Discussion techniques that work

Finally, the moment arrives. After careful Bible study and prayer, the time comes when it is your turn to lead the discussion. The most significant thing you can remember is you do not have to be an expert, a walking biblical encyclopedia with all the answers. Your task, as leader, is not to provide the answers, but to guide the group as they search for them. It means encouraging each one to contribute the spiritual insights he has learned during his private study. Out of the interaction will come additional truths hidden, till then, in God's Word.

A leader must decide not to dominate the discussion. The diagrams below illustrate this clearly.

The flow of discussion in an effective group looks like this:

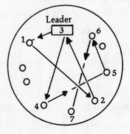

and not like this:

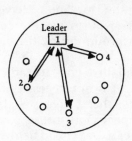

Here are four discussion techniques that work:

1. Extending:
   "What else can you add to that?"
   "Could you explain that more fully?"

2. Clarifying:
   "What do you mean by that?"
   "Could you rephrase that statement?"

3. Justifying:
   "Would you explain that?"
   "What reason do you give for that?"

4. Redirecting:
   "Mary, what do you think?"
   "What do you notice, John?"[13]

D. Some hints to success

Before coming to the session where you are scheduled to be the leader, spend some time alone with God. Spiritual leadership involves far more than intellectual knowledge or an understanding of group dynamics. Your Bible study group is part of God's plan to take His message of salvation to the world. Ask the Lord to enable you to be at your best and to be sensitive to the needs of those who attend.

You can trust the Holy Spirit. He will fill you with His presence, enabling you to be the means by which He can work in your group during the meeting where you are the leader.

Keep in mind that you are not commissioned to defend the truth. It is not necessary for you to correct every heretical idea that is suggested. Let the Bible speak for itself, and expect God to use you more effectively than you have ever experienced before.

7

How to . . .

In this chapter, we consider these practical areas, all beginning with "How to . . ."

. . . ask questions
. . . stay on track
. . . handle the talkative
. . . involve the quiet people
. . . handle silence
. . . respond to difficult questions
. . . deal with gossip

A. How to ask questions

Leaders ask questions. That is part of their task as a Bible study leader. Good leaders ask good questions—questions that spark discussion, prompt inquiry, and encourage personal involvement.

Questions serve three major purposes in group discussion:

1. Uncover the facts
2. Explore the relationship between bits of truth
3. Reveal the impact of truth on the participating individuals

Since the major goal of a small group Bible study is the intersection of scriptural truth and human personality, a skillful use of questions is of major importance. Here are some guidelines that will help the leader use questions more effectively.

1. Avoid using closed-ended questions, that is, questions that can be answered yes or no.
2. Be prepared to wait for an answer.
3. Listen attentively.
4. Use questions that deal with feelings as well as fact.
5. Deal with people's true interests.
6. Answer questions with questions.
7. Learn when and how to use direct and indirect questions. A direct question causes a person to take an open stand and declare a position. Indirect questions are not as personal nor as threatening.
8. Avoid questions that assume an answer.
9. Use questions that focus on a specific item.[14]

It is most helpful to ask only one question at a time. If a question is asked of a specific individual, make sure that the person is able to answer it, in order to avoid embarrassment.

B. How to stay on track

One of the most challenging aspects of leadership is to find the balance between a full discussion of the scripture passage and time-wasting conversation about irrelevant issues. One reason for encouraging the group to make a commitment to each other is found here. When the group has established its own goals, the leader can remind them gently that they are wandering away from their commitment.

If an answer or comment is clearly off track, the leader can respond by asking: "What verse are you referring to?" Or, "Where do you find that in the passage?"

"Our goal is to make people feel comfortable while at the same time handling the text with integrity."[15]

"If someone asks a question that isn't relevant to the study and it interrupts the flow, have a paper and pencil handy and jot it down. Tell the person you will discuss it later with him. Usually the Lord will answer the question during the study and the person will feel no need to pursue it."[16]

C. How to handle the talkative

Occasionally, someone will dominate the group by talking too much. Perhaps they feel that they are better informed than anyone else, or they may see the Bible study as an opportunity to convert everyone to their doctrinal position. For some, the group is their only social contact. They enjoy the rare privilege of conversing with anyone who is interested.

Yet, the leader has a responsibility to the group to give everyone a chance to participate. Sometimes the "talkers" can be slowed down by deliberately refusing to have eye contact with them. As you ask a question, look at someone else in the group, as if you expect them to answer.

On other occasions, react to the talker by asking, "What do the rest of you think?"

In some extreme cases, you can break the pattern by saying, "I am going to ask a question and then we are going to go around the circle. Each person is to give an answer, and the answer cannot be more than one sentence long." Then arrange it so the talker is neither the first nor the last to respond.

D. How to involve the quiet people

Begin by establishing through your conduct that you consider every answer important. Listen to people as they talk; look them in the eye. This will help the insecure who do not answer from the fear that they will be embarrassed.

Establish eye contact with these quiet ones. By your obvious desire to hear what they have to say, encourage them to speak. Ask them simple questions. Inquire how they feel about what is being discussed. Gently urge them to be involved. Let them know you value what they have to say. Soon they, too, will be involved.

E. How to handle silence

Listen!

Listen to the silence; it can speak to you.

Our Quaker friends have discovered a great truth. We could profit by their advice when they say, "Go into the silence and listen."

Some of the most meaningful moments in a group Bible study are the quiet times. If you are not threatened as the leader, the group will not be uneasy, either.

The Holy Spirit may need some quiet times in order to deal with each individual on a very personal level. Sometimes people need a chance to think about the truth that is being discussed. So when silence comes, don't panic. Just listen.

F. How to respond to difficult questions

"I don't know" is always an acceptable answer.

"Let's see what the Bible says" is another good response.

If, after a period of discussion, you are making no progress toward an answer, you can say to the group, "Let's write this question down and see if we can find an answer this week. Next time we meet we will spend the first 10 minutes discussing what we have learned."

Then, when you meet again, restrict your discussion

to the agreed-upon time period. Some leaders control this by setting a kitchen timer and, when it rings, saying, "Our time is up. Let's move on to our study for today."

G. How to deal with gossip

Gossip must be stopped, immediately. Once again, the value of the group commitment is apparent. As noted earlier, when there are group members who are not church members, it is less likely that people will gossip.

Be alert that improper information is not revealed under the guise of a prayer request. It is not necessary for the group to know all the details nor even the full names of people in order to pray for them.

As God's servant, be bold in the Lord and stop gossip before it hurts people or damages the fellowship in the group.

Keep in mind that problems can either be opportunities to succeed or occasions for failure. Our attitude toward them determines the result.

8

Learning to Pray

In this chapter, we discuss the third major component in a successful study group: prayer.

These aspects will be considered:
  A. Learning to pray
  B. Forms of prayer

A. Learning to pray

Prayer is not an automatic action given to the believer at the new birth as breathing is given to the infant. Prayer is more like walking. It is a skill to be learned. The more one practices it, the more proficient he becomes.

Learning to pray aloud in a group can be a frightening experience. On occasion, there have been people who have avoided a small-group Bible study because they were afraid they would be asked to pray. When leadership is sensitive to these legitimate fears, plans can be made to protect the people who are inexperienced in praying, and assist them in learning how to pray.

In the next section, we present some ideas to deal with the concerns expressed in these paragraphs.

B. Forms of prayer

There comes a time in every Bible study session when the group ought to pray together. Periods of quiet meditation are valuable, but there is no substitute for the vocal expression of our thanksgiving and petitions.

But what about those who have never prayed in public? One skilled group leader says,

> In every study I lead there comes a time when I gently, but firmly inform the group that we are going to pray out loud. After the panic leaves their faces, I explain.
>
> "Let's go around the circle, starting with me, and each of us thank God for something. You can just say one word, one thing you are thankful for." Then I start,
>
> "Dear Lord, we bring to You this morning just one thing out of the many You give us and we thank You for it. Lord, I thank You for my husband." The next person says, "the sunshine," and the next may say, "my baby," and so on around the room. When it comes to me again, I say, "Amen."[17]

Later, single words can be lengthened to single sentences, and finally short paragraphs.

A highly effective way to pray in a group like this is "conversationally." Conversational prayer includes these facets:

1. Each group member who wishes to do so tells God frankly what he has to say to Him.
2. Praying is done in a conversational tone—directly, simply, briefly.
3. Only one thing is prayed about at a time—a personal concern.
4. Once a group member has introduced his concern, at least one other member, and probably several, by audible prayer "covers with love" their friend's concern.

5. Then there is a waiting in silence before God. Each person listens to what God is saying to him.
6. Following the listening period, another member may introduce a personal concern in prayer. The prayer time continues with members feeling free to pray several times.

9

"How to Use This Study Guide,"

This chapter contains the introduction that is printed in the front of each copy of the Beacon Small-Group Bible Study Series.

HOW TO USE THIS STUDY GUIDE

BEFORE YOU BEGIN THIS ADVENTURE IN A SMALL-GROUP BIBLE STUDY... READ THESE PAGES OF INTRODUCTION

God has created us with a basic human need for close personal relationships. This may take place *as you gather in a small group* to apply the Bible to your life.

I. WHAT SHOULD HAPPEN IN SMALL-GROUP BIBLE STUDY?

"They devoted themselves to the apostles' teaching and to the fellowship . . . and to prayer" (Acts 2:42, NIV).

Each group is different . . . yet all should include three kinds of activity—

DISCUSSION BIBLE STUDY
SHARING EXPERIENCES
PRAYING TOGETHER

The time you spend in Bible study, sharing, and praying will vary according to the needs of the group. However, do not neglect any of these activities.

The BIBLE contains God's plan for our salvation and gives us His guidance for our lives. Keep the focus on God speaking to you from His Word.

On the other hand, just to learn Bible facts will make little difference in a person's life. To give opportunity for persons to *share* what the truth means to them is to let God come alive today. Learn to listen intently to others and to share what you feel God's Word is saying to you.

Allow time for PRAYER. Personal communion with God is essential in all fruitful Bible studies. Determine to make prayer more than a "nod to God" at the beginning or end of each session. As members participate in sincere, unhurried prayer—you will be amazed how God's power will meet needs in your group . . . today!

II. HOW TO BEGIN YOUR FIRST SESSION TO-GETHER

The leader of a new group may wish to prepare name tags with first and last names large enough to be seen plainly.

It is important to order the *Beacon Small-Group Bible Study Guides* and give one to each person in your group at the beginning of the first session. Pass out the guides and refer the group to this section of the introductory guidance. Then ask each person to consider the following:

44

One thing I would like to gain from sharing in this time together is:

Rank the following in order, using number one (1) to indicate the most important and number five (5) as least important.

( ) 1. Learning to know Bible truths and apply them to my life

( ) 2. A chance to begin all over again in my spiritual life

( ) 3. To grow in my personal faith in God

( ) 4. To deepen my friendships with others in the group as we study the Word together

( ) 5. Other purpose _____

Take time to go around the group to introduce yourselves. Then let each member share what he or she would like to gain from this Bible study by filling in the blanks and by discussing this statement: I choose _____ as number one because _____. I put _____ as number five because _____.

At this point, pause for prayer, asking God to bless this Bible study and especially to meet the needs just expressed by the members of the group.

III. A KEY TO SUCCESS . . . MAKE A GROUP COMMITMENT

What should be included in the group commitment? At the first or second meeting, read the following points, then discuss each one separately.

1. Agree to make regular attendance a top priority of the group.

   Commitment to each other is of vital importance.

2. Where and when will the group meet?

   Decide on a place and time. The place can be always in the same home or in a different home each week, at a restaurant, or in any other relaxed setting. Plan to be on time.

The time _____ The place(s) _____
How often?　　(　) Every week
　　　　　　　(　) Every other week

3. Decide on the length of the meetings.

   The minimum should be one hour; maximum two hours. Whatever you decide, be sure to dismiss on time. If they wish, some may remain after the group is dismissed. Length _____.

4. Decide whether the same person will lead each session, or if you prefer a group coordinator and a rotation of leaders.

   Our leader or coordinator is _____.

5. Agree together that there shall be no criticism of others.

   Also no discussion of church problems and no gossip shall be expressed in the group. Our goal in this Bible study is to affirm and to build up each other.

6. Decide on the maximum number of people your group should contain. When this maximum is reached, you will encourage the formation of a new group. We want our group to grow. New-comers, as they understand and agree to the group commitment, will keep things fresh. Feel free to bring a friend. Whenever our group reaches an average attendance of _____ persons for three consecutive weeks, we will plan to begin a new group.

   Do not become a closed clique. This would eventually lead to an ingrown group. Our goal is outreach, friendliness, and openness to new people.

7. Our time together as a group will be more fulfilling if all of us complete our personal Bible reading before we come together again.

   Are group members deciding to make this commitment to personal Bible reading and reflection?

   _____

8. Decide on the number of times you wish to meet before you reevaluate the areas of your commitment. (Enter below.)

MY COMMITMENT TO CHRIST
and THE MEMBERS OF MY GROUP

I agree to meet with others in my group for _____ weeks to become a learner in God's Word.

I commit myself to give priority to our group gatherings, to a thoughtful reading of the Bible passages to be explored, and to love and support others in my group.

Signed _____ Date _____

IV. GUIDELINES

1. Get acquainted with each other; be on a first-name basis.
2. Each one bring your Bible and keep it open during the study.
3. As you read the Bible passage, each person may ask himself three questions:
   —What does the passage say?
   —What does it mean?
   —What does it mean to me?
4. Stay with the Bible passage before you. Moving to numerous cross-references may confuse a person new to the Bible.

5. Avoid technical theological words. Make sure any theological terms you use are explained clearly to the group.

6. The leader or coordinator should prepare for each session by studying the passage thoroughly before the group meeting, including reviewing the questions in the study guide. In the group study, the leader should ask the study guide questions, giving adequate time for the discussion of each question.

Remember, the leader is not to lecture on what he has learned from studying, but should lead the group in discovering for themselves what the Scripture says. In sharing your discoveries, say, "The Scripture says . . . ," rather than, "My church says . . ."

7. The leader should not talk too much and should not answer his own questions. The leader should give opportunity for anyone who wishes to speak. Redirect some of the questions asked back to the group. As members get to know each other better, the discussion will move more freely.

The flow of discussion in an effective group looks like this:

And not like this:

8. In a loving but firm manner maintain the guidelines for the group. Discourage overtalkative members from monopolizing the time. If necessary, the leader may speak privately to the overtalkative one and enlist his aid in encouraging all to participate. Direct questions to all persons in the group.

9. Plan to reserve some time at the end of each session for prayer together. Encourage any who wish to lead out in spoken prayer in response to the Scripture truths or personal needs expressed in the group.

   Even if you do not complete all the study for that particular meeting, *take time to pray.* The main purpose of group Bible study is not just to cover all the facts, but to apply the truth to human lives. It will be exciting to discover your life growing and changing as you encourage each other in Christ's love.

   A highly effective way to pray in a group like this is "conversationally." Conversational prayer includes:

   a. Each group member who wishes to do so tells God frankly what he has to say to Him.
   b. Praying done in a conversational tone—directly, simply, briefly.
   c. Only one thing is prayed about at a time—a personal concern.
   d. Once a group member has introduced his concern, at least one other member, and probably several, by audible prayer "covers with love" their friend's concern.
   e. Then there is a waiting in silence before God. Each person listens to what God is saying to him.

f. Following the listening period, another member may introduce a personal concern in prayer. The prayer time continues with members feeling free to pray several times.

V. AIDS FOR YOUR STUDY

For Group Leaders

You will find helpful *How to Lead a Small-Group Bible Study*, by Gene Van Note, available from the Beacon Hill Press of Kansas City, Box 527, Kansas City, MO 64141.

For Leaders, Coordinators, and Participants

Bible commentaries should not be taken with you to the study period, but it is often helpful to refer to sound commentaries and expositions in your preparation. We recommend:

Beacon Bible Commentary
Volume (according to the Bible book to be studied)
Beacon Bible Expositions
Volume (according to the Bible book to be studied)

It is also helpful to refer occasionally to some general Bible resources, such as:

Know Your New Testament, by Ralph Earle
Halley's Bible Handbook

The above resources are available from Beacon Hill Press of Kansas City or from your publishing house.

—This Introduction by Wil M. Spaite

Notes

1. Lawrence O. Richards, *69 Ways to Start a Study Group and Keep It Growing* (Grand Rapids: Zondervan Publishing House, 1973), pp. 11-12.

2. *Ibid.,* p. 11.

3. Gladys Hunt, *It's Alive* (Wheaton, Ill.: Harold Shaw Publishers, 1971), p. 33.

4. *Lead Out* (Colorado Springs: NavPress, 1974), pp. 7-8.

5. Hunt, *It's Alive,* p. 52.

6. *Ibid.,* p. 45.

7. *Ibid.,* p. 39.

8. Adapted from Richards, *69 Ways,* pp. 12-13.

9. Hunt, *It's Alive,* p. 31.

10. *Lead Out,* p. 70.

11. Norma Spande, *Your Guide to Successful Home Bible Studies* (Nashville: Thomas Nelson Publishers, 1979), p. 13.

12. Hunt, *It's Alive,* pp. 72-73.

13. *Lead Out,* p. 39.

14. *Ibid.,* pp. 48-52.

15. Hunt, *It's Alive,* p. 69.

16. Spande, *Your Guide,* p. 114.

17. *Ibid.,* p. 96.